Lamborghini Aventador

JULIA GARSTECKI

BLACK RABBIT BOOKS

Bolt is published by Black Rabbit Books
P.O. Box 3263, Mankato, Minnesota, 56002.
www.blackrabbitbooks.com
Copyright © 2020 Black Rabbit Books

Marysa Storm, editor; Catherine Cates,
interior designer; Grant Gould, cover designer;
Omay Ayres, photo researcher

All rights reserved. No part of this book may be reproduced,
stored in a retrieval system or transmitted in any form or by any means,
electronic, mechanical, photocopying, recording, or otherwise, without written
permission from the publisher.

Library of Congress Cataloging-in-Publication Data
Names: Garstecki, Julia, author.
Title: Lamborghini Aventador / by Julia Garstecki.
Description: Mankato, Minnesota : Black Rabbit Books, [2020] | Series: Bolt.
Epic cars | Includes index. | Audience: Ages 9-12. | Audience: Grades 4 to 6.
Identifiers: LCCN 2018015185 (print) | LCCN 2018019363 (ebook) |
ISBN 9781680728460 (e-book) | ISBN 9781680728385 (library binding) |
ISBN 9781644660379 (paperback)
Subjects: LCSH: Aventador automobile–Juvenile literature.
Classification: LCC TL215.L33 (ebook) | LCC TL215.L33 G37 2020 (print) |
DDC 629.222/2-dc23
LC record available at https://lccn.loc.gov/2018015185

Special thanks to Justin Storm for his help with this book.

Printed in the United States. 1/19

Image Credits
Alamy: David Michielsen, 25; commons.wikimedia.org: Alexandre Prévot, 12 (btm); dieselstation.com: Automobili Lamborghini, 20–21; images-free.net: Automobili Lamborghini, 19; lamborghinipalmbeach.com: Lamborghini Palm Beach, 14 (colors); media.lamborghini.com: Automobili Lamborghini, Cover (car); Lamborghini Media Center, 1, 4–5, 6 (top), 8–9, 11, 12 (top), 14 (stitching), 14–15, 16 (top, middle), 23, 24 (btm), 26, 28–29, 31; Shutterstock: AmorSt-Photographer, 24 (top); Elenamiv, Cover (bkgd); josefkubes, 3; Max Earey, 16 (btm); meunierd, 6 (btm); pio3, 32; slava296, 26–27
Every effort has been made to contact copyright holders for material reproduced in this book. Any omissions will be rectified in subsequent printings if notice is given to the publisher.

Contents

CHAPTER 1
Racing Down
the Road............4

CHAPTER 2
Design............10

CHAPTER 3
Power and
Performance..........18

CHAPTER 4
An Epic Car.........29

Other Resources............30

CHAPTER 1

Racing Down the Road

A man flips open a bright red cover. The cover protects a start button. It's not a button to start a rocket, though. It's to start a Lamborghini Aventador. With a press of the button, the car springs to life. The driver steps on the gas pedal. Roaring, the car races down the street. Within seconds, the flashy car is out of sight.

The name Aventador comes from a famous Spanish bull. Like the bull, the car is powerful.

A Sleek Car

Lamborghini released the first Aventador in 2011. Like other Lambos, it is low, wide, and fast. The company has made many versions of the car.

In 2016, Lambo revealed the Aventador S. It has more **horsepower** than the Aventador. It has better handling and **agility** too. It's also more stylish.

PARTS OF AN AVENTADOR S

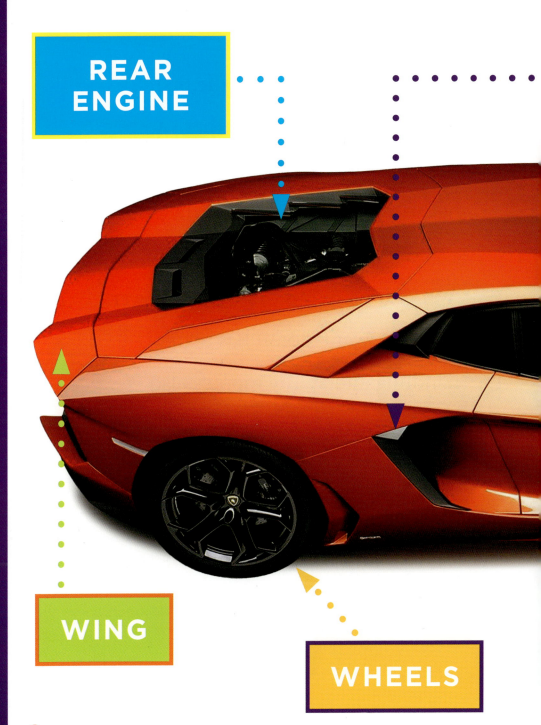

VENTS

WIDE, LOW BODY

CHAPTER 2

Drivers can buy an Aventador S as a roadster or coupe. Both have the classic Lambo look. They're sleek and wedge-shaped. The biggest difference between them is the roof. The driver can remove the roadster's roof. It fits in the front trunk.

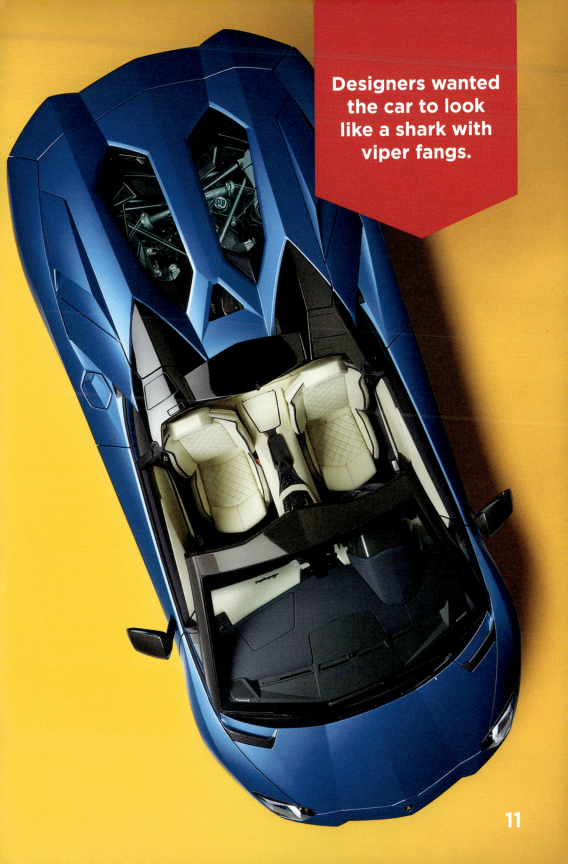

Designers wanted the car to look like a shark with viper fangs.

Personalized

Picking the model is just the beginning. The Aventador S comes in 39 colors. There are six colors for brake **calipers**. Buyers can pick different rim styles and colors too. And that's just the outside! There are many options inside. Buyers can choose seat colors. They select thread colors too.

The car has scissor doors. They open upward, pivoting like scissors.

MANY OPTIONS

Drivers have many options when buying an Aventador S Coupe.

39 EXTERIOR COLORS

13 STITCHING COLORS

6
BRAKE CALIPER COLORS

3
ENGINE BONNET STYLES

15

Carbon Fiber

Many parts of the Aventador S are carbon fiber. This material is both light and strong. Drivers can have some of those carbon fiber parts visible. They can also order carbon fiber features. Carbon fiber parts give the car a **unique** look.

CHAPTER 3

Power and Performance

The Aventador S has a 6.5-liter V-12 engine. It's designed for max speed. The car has 740 metric horsepower. It rockets up to 217 miles (349 kilometers) per hour.

COMPARING TOP SPEEDS

2018 Bugatti Chiron

2018 Aventador S

2018 McLaren 720S

2018 Ferrari 812 Superfast

miles per hour

261 (420 km)

217 (349 km)

212 (341 km)

211 (340 km)

200 210 220 230 240 250 260

Strada means "street" in Italian. *Corsa* means "track."

Technology

The Aventador S has four driving modes. They are STRADA, SPORT, CORSA, and EGO. STRADA is best for daily driving. It saves on fuel. Drivers use SPORT for sporty driving. It's best for curved roads. CORSA gives drivers the most control. It is best for tracks. EGO lets drivers choose specific settings.

Specialized Steering

The Aventador S has four-wheel steering. This steering helps drivers have the best ride possible. At slower speeds, the back wheels turn slightly in the opposite direction of the front. This action improves agility. The car can race around curves. At higher speeds, the back wheels turn with the front. This action increases the car's **stability**. The ride is smoother.

The Aventador S has 130 percent more front downforce than the Aventador. Downforce presses a car to the ground. It increases stability at high speeds.

Aventador Horsepower

AVENTADOR

700 metric horsepower

AVENTADOR S

740 metric horsepower

750 metric horsepower

AVENTADOR SV

The Aventador SV

Some drivers want an even sportier and stronger car. The SV is for them. SV stands for Superveloce. *Veloce* means "fast" in Italian. This car has even more horsepower. It takes less time to reach top speeds.

By the Numbers

AVENTADOR S

2 TOTAL SEATING

79.9 INCHES (203 CENTIMETERS) **WIDTH** WITHOUT MIRRORS

ESTIMATED HIGHWAY MILEAGE

about **17** miles (27 km) per gallon

In 2018, Lamborghini revealed the Aventador SVJ. It's even sportier than the SV. The car has 770 metric horsepower.

CHAPTER 4

An Epic Car

The Aventador came out in 2011. It's only gotten better over the years. Future versions will be faster. They'll be more stylish. These cars will impress drivers for years to come!

GLOSSARY

agility (uh-JIL-i-tee)—the ability to move quickly and easily

bonnet (BON-it)—a car hood or covering

caliper (KAL-uh-per)—a device used to press a brake pad against the sides of a brake rotor

carbon fiber (KAR-buhn FAHY-bur)—a very strong, lightweight material

horsepower (HORS-pow-uhr)—a unit used to measure the power of engines

mileage (MAHY-lij)—the average number of miles a vehicle will travel on a gallon of gasoline

pivot (PIV-uht)—to turn on or around a central point

stability (stuh-BIL-i-tee)—being able to remain steady and stable

unique (yoo-NEEK)—very special or unusual

LEARN MORE

BOOKS

Cockerham, Paul W. *Lamborghini: A Fusion of Technology and Power*. Speed Rules! Inside the World's Hottest Cars. Broomall, PA: Mason Crest, 2018.

Cruz, Calvin. *Lamborghini Aventador*. Car Crazy. Minneapolis: Bellwether Media, 2016.

Kingston, Seth. *The History of Lamborghinis*. Under the Hood. New York: PowerKids Press, 2019.

WEBSITES

Lamborghini Aventador
www.lamborghini.com/en-en/models/aventador

Lamborghini Aventador Reviews
www.caranddriver.com/lamborghini/aventador

Lamborghini Car Configurator
configurator.lamborghini.com/configurator/?lang=eng&country=it

INDEX

A
acceleration, 27

B
brakes, 15

C
carbon fiber, 17

costs, 27

D
designs, 7, 8–9, 10, 11, 13, 14–15, 17, 26–27

driving modes, 21

E
engines, 8, 15, 18

H
history, 7, 29

horsepower, 7, 18, 24–25, 28

S
speeds, 18–19

steering, 22